Test Your Cat's IQ
GENIUS EDITION

SIMON HOLLAND
ILLUSTRATIONS BY
ERICA SALCEDO SAIZ

In memory of Rupert, the Über-Cat.
And to Smudge, who always scores well.

Text copyright © 2016 Simon Holland
Illustrations by Erica Salcedo Saiz
Cover and interior design: Rosamund Saunders
Cat-sultant: Carron Brown
Cover images © Shutterstock

Skyhorse Publishing books may be purchased
in bulk at special discounts for sales promotion,
corporate gifts, fund-raising, or educational
purposes. Special editions can also be created to
specifications. For details, contact the Special Sales
Department, Skyhorse Publishing, 307 West 36th
Street, 11th Floor, New York, NY 10018 or
info@skyhorsepublishing.com.

Visit our website at www.skyhorsepublishing.com.

10 9 8 7 6 5 4 3 2 1

Library of Congress Cataloging-in-Publication Data
is available on file.

ISBN: 978-1-51070487-9

Printed in China

MIX
Paper from
responsible sources
FSC™ C007454

FSC™ is a non-profit international organisation established
to promote the responsible management of the world's
forests. Products carrying the FSC label are independently
certified to assure consumers that they come from forests
that are managed to meet the social, economic and
ecological needs of present and future generations.

Contents

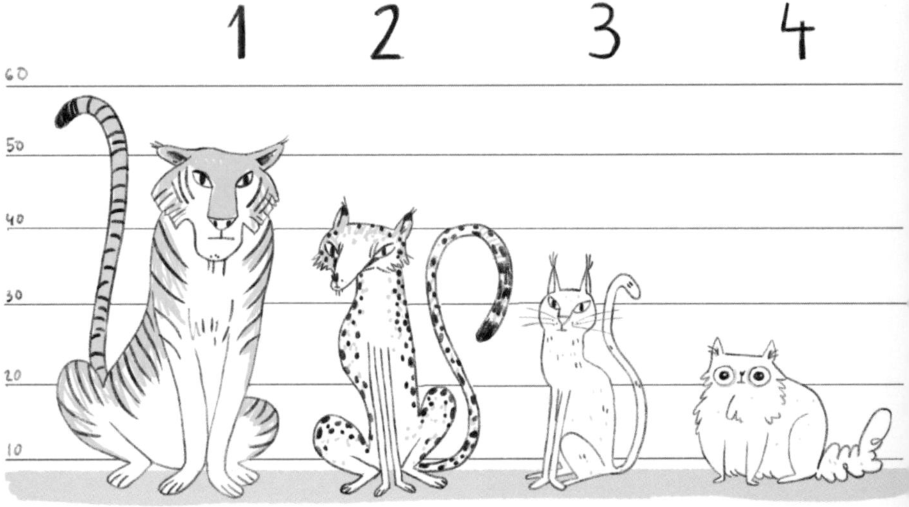
1
2
3
4
60
50
40
30
20
10

Introduction

It's fair to say that cats have always had a head start on humans. The distant ancestors of cats appeared about 30 million years ago, while ours came about only two or three million years ago—with modern humans dragging their heels (or the backs of their hands?) until their eventual appearance on the evolutionary scene roughly 200,000 years ago.

We now know that humans have been living with cats, or keeping them as pets, for over 12,000 years. So by the time of the ancient Egyptians—who elevated cats to a godlike status about 3,600 years ago—cats had already had more than enough time to get their paws under the antique coffee tables of some of the most successful human civilizations in history.

When cats and humans first crossed paths, it would have been obvious to cats that humans were there for the taking. These docile, pliable, manipulable mammals were lolloping around on two legs—which seemed to be some kind of "amazing novelty"—and were far too impressed by fire to notice the feline forms slipping tasty marshmallows from their campfire sticks.

"At last," thought the cats, "our days of foraging and fending for ourselves are over. We've finally found a species gullible enough to do it all for us."

But over the last 10,000 years or so, maybe domestic cats have become a little complacent. And maybe there just aren't enough challenges anymore . . . not enough stresses left in feline life to keep cats shimmying up the evolutionary scale.

It's time for them to start thinking outside the basket, and here's how you—the cat owner—can help.

With the aid of this book, you can set for your pet a series of tasks and activities that will reveal the complex nature of their existing skills and abilities. At the same time— who knows?—these challenges may also have the domino effect of boosting their brilliance and teasing some new feline adaptations out of their evolutionary slumber . . . so that cats can conquer the modern world all over again.

Measuring Your Cat's Ingenuity

Testing your cat for signs of intelligence, ingenuity and originality can be great fun, because it also teases out the facets of your pet's personality. Cats are not always as predictable as other animals, because—although domesticated—they've retained little bits and pieces of their wildness, their independence, their *esprit d'aventure*. They make decisions based on how they feel, or how much they feel they can get away with. Perhaps this is what makes them such fascinating and entertaining animals to have around: they would probably prefer to please themselves before they pleased you, but in doing so they provide something of a comical nature documentary that you can try and capture within the confines of your own home and/or backyard.

Making the Most of the Tests

Okay. So someone's bought you this book as a gift or Christmas stocking stuffer, and you've giggled while flicking through it, but at the back of your mind you're thinking, "This one's heading straight for the downstairs bathroom." Hold on just a second. The more time you dedicate to these tests, the more they can work for you in trying to decode the walking enigma that stalks your domicile.

If you're in the mood for a few quick-fire, fun games to play with your animals, you'll find plenty of them in this book and you can notch up all your cat's scores for a rainy day (when you'll have time for some of the more searching activities). Other tests require you to play out the activity repeatedly (in order to get the clearest result) or over the course of several days. In short, this book is for life—not just for Christmas.

As for your cat ... many of the tests involve the cat engaging in "solo" behavior, while some involve other cats or animals. And here comes the rub: some of the most interesting tests focus on the ways in which your cat interacts with, tests, and manipulates you. In fact, some of the biggest scores can be achieved by a cat that is adept at getting you to behave in ways that make its life a virtual nirvana.

Have a stopwatch or smartphone at the ready, as some of the activities are timed tests. So, once again, you may want to retest your cat—perhaps over the course of a few days or weeks—to see if the animal is able to improve on its performance.

In some of the activities, multiple points are available for cats that meet the requirements of the tests in different ways. These "multiple score" or "bonus score" areas are clearly indicated, so please only award these extra points where applicable. If you decide to cheat, then you're only cheating your pet (and, ultimately, yourself).

Categories of Genius

In order to make these tests as pseudo-academically sound as possible, they have been divided into five thematic areas.

PHYSICAL TESTS

This set of activities examines the ways in which your cat uses its body to achieve a distinct advantage in its surroundings. So these are not just tests of strength and agility, they are also tests of the animal's cunning and creativity.

TERRITORIAL TESTS

Here's where you can measure the balance (or imbalance) between your cat's natural instincts and its ability to tailor them to the rigors of rural, urban, or suburban life.

METEOROLOGY AND CAT COSMOLOGY

After measuring your cat's physical and territorial awareness, you can see how well it copes with factors that it cannot control easily—namely the weather and the broader interactions of visible and invisible matter in the universe.

PSYCHOLOGICAL TESTS

This is what the book is really building up to—a measure of what's truly going on beyond those bright eyes. Your cat's modes of behavior are also modes of self-expression and indicators of mood. Let's take a really close look at them.

SUPERNATURAL TESTS

At first glance, this section looks like it's just for fun . . . But is it? Analyzing your cat's subtle quirks may uncover a few connections with the paranormal—and send a few shivers down your spine as well. So don't be a skeptic—your pet could be a gateway to the spirit world, and just imagine how cool (and potentially lucrative) that would be!

Scoring tips and conclusions are given on pages 125–127, so that you can analyze your pet's performance in each of the above categories and thus compile its physical and psychological profile. You can also identify the areas in which the animal might be able to do better in the future.

• General note (for all sections): try not to let your cat know that it is being tested. It probably won't like the idea of being assessed, and so will not offer its cooperation voluntarily. Some stealth may be required.

Chapter One

PHYSICAL TESTS

House cats are domesticated animals, but they've cunningly retained a little bit of their wild side—just enough to keep you on your toes. Cats may live in your home, but they do so purely for their own convenience. They've adapted to the home environment, but they can take it or leave it, depending on their immediate and ever-changing needs. A closer examination of their physical behavior can reveal all kinds of hidden nuances in your cat's ability to manipulate not only its environment but you as well.

The following physical tests and activities will help you measure this level of domestic adaptation. Score each section carefully, repeating the experiment—as and when necessary—to achieve an average score that truly reflects the general attitude of your pet.

Test of the True Cat

Is your cat genuine? Is it a true cat or some kind of charlatan *chat* or feline faker? Contrary to what all the experts say, there is in fact only one way to find out.

In full view of your cat, place a small object (e.g., a coin or a pencil) near the edge of a table or other high-altitude surface where there are few (if any) other objects. Grab a stopwatch and see how long it takes for your cat to bat that object into oblivion.

If your cat is truly a cat, it will knock that object off the edge at some point after becoming aware of it. The speed of response is key: the faster, the more feline.

☐ No response **NIL POINTS**

☐ 5 minutes **1 POINT**

☐ 1 minute **2 POINTS**

☐ 30 seconds **3 POINTS**

☐ 10 seconds **4 POINTS**

☐ Less than 5 seconds **5 POINTS**

2

Engaging with Confined Spaces: a Metaphysical Challenge

The pacific octopus has a 13-foot-wide arm span, and yet it can slip through a gap no wider than a tennis ball. Generally, cats can squeeze themselves through some pretty tight fissures (sometimes as narrow as 3 inches), but it's time to find out exactly what their attitude is to the metaphysical problem of the confined space.

When presented with a diverse range of boxes, cases, and containers, your cat:

☐ Takes one look at them and then retires to the couch.
1 POINT

☐ Checks each box for traces of food before entering.
2 POINTS

☐ Slips into the box or case that has the most luxurious lining. **3 POINTS**

☐ Chooses the smallest receptacle and doesn't leave it alone until it has succeeded in pushing its whole body into it.
4 POINTS

☐ Tries each container in turn until the optimum cat-to-box comfort ratio has been identified. **5 POINTS**

☐ Fetches a set of laser-guided measuring instruments and proceeds to carry out a structural survey of each container.
5 POINTS

3

Stance Decoder

In order to tune in to the moods and intelligence of your cat, you need to know how to interpret its various poses and stances. The stances listed here are physical messages transmitted from your cat to the other beings in its general vicinity.

MULTIPLE AWARD

Be honest: tick the stances you've seen your cat adopt on a daily basis and total the scores accordingly. Do not include any postures that are not a regular or daily occurrence.

☐ THE TEAPOT: paws tucked under, tail tucked around, all bunched up with face forward and back curved—all the cat needs is a handle. The teapot stance serves you a tepid cup of disappointment. You clearly could have done better with that thing you should have noticed/should have done.
2 POINTS

☐ THE REVERSE TEAPOT: not only have you not done what your cat asked you to do, but you've overstepped the mark. The rear end of the pot is presented. No cup of warmth can be poured. No eye contact. You're locked out. **3 POINTS**

☐ THE PARALLELOGRAM: this is a sleeping or relaxing position that denotes complete relaxation, serenity, and personal security. Note how the forelimbs lie in a perfectly parallel formation in respect of the hind limbs. **2 POINTS**

teapot

reverse teapot

parallelogram

☐ THE CHAISE LONGUE PLAY-ALONG: when a cat lies on its side like this, with at least one forelimb outstretched, it's ready to be playful and interactive. **2 POINTS**

☐ THE OPEN BOOK OF DECEPTION: one of the more ambiguous postures, this "belly up and exposed" stance exudes a feeling of confidence and contentment, but it's also a defensive posture, allowing the animal to take a nifty swipe at you if you penetrate its aura of pleasure with your interfering mitts. **3 POINTS**

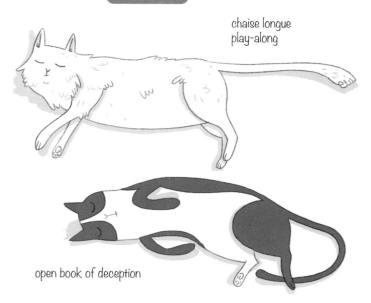

chaise longue play-along

open book of deception

4

Tail Semaphore

Thanks to so-called evolutionary progress, we humans have lost our tail, and this is a problem. We can no longer comprehend the full range of signals that animals send out by virtue of their versatile rear appendages. But with a little care and attention, we can try and understand the basic messages contained in the subtle flexings of a domestic cat's tail.

MULTIPLE AWARD

If your cat uses its tail to control or manipulate you in certain ways, then it deserves some points for each of the stylings below—so long as they are employed on either a regular or day-to-day basis.

☐ THE NIP AND TUCK: when a cat has its tail hidden beneath its undercarriage, it's either fearful of something or generally ill at ease. **I POINT**

☐ THE BURNING FUSE: a fast side-to-side or twitching motion could indicate that your cat is highly irritated, or frightened, and about to lash out. **I POINT**

☐ TUNE ME IN: this straight, upward tail shows that your cat is happy, confident, and relatively pleased to see you.
2 POINTS

☐ RIDDLE ME THIS: this question-mark-shaped tail is indeed asking a question: "Are you up for some feline interaction?" It denotes a mood of openness and playfulness. **2 POINTS**

nip and tuck

burning fuse

tune me in

riddle me this

☐ THE SLOW ASSASSIN: this tail denotes the deep, lucid intelligence of a Bond villain. It moves slowly, from side to side, to mask the fact that the cat is about to attack another animal, person, or object. (Note: may be combined with the bouffant, below.) **3 POINTS**

BONUS SECTION: If you have more than one cat, or your cat regularly interacts with other felines, then your pet could be eligible for the following bonus points:

☐ THE BOUFFANT (AKA THE INCREDIBLE HULK): suddenly, it looks as if your cat has had a wash and blow-dry. It has arched its back and puffed out its tail to make it look bigger and more powerful in front of other cats.
3 POINTS

☐ THE WRAP-AROUND: cats wrap their tails around each other to show that they are members of an exclusive club known as the FTU (Feline Trade Union), an institution that automatically blackballs humans. **2 POINTS**

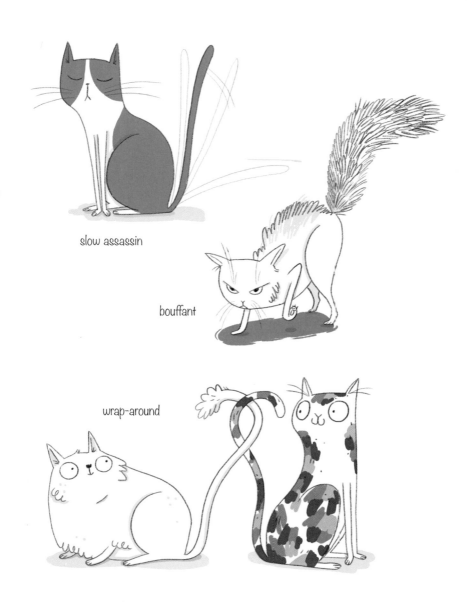

slow assassin

bouffant

wrap-around

5

The Leap of Faith

From a feline perspective, every jump from floor to table is a journey into the unknown. It's a risky business. There's no way of knowing what's on that table and what the landing conditions will be like. So this is the perfect way to find out how foolhardy, happy-go-lucky, and/or courageous your cat is.

Set out various tables, of different heights, and add or subtract different objects from them on a day-to-day basis. Observe your cat (from a hidden location) as it leaps onto these foreign surfaces. After a few days, you'll be able to judge its performance by ticking the relevant boxes below.

☐ My cat can only land safely on an uncluttered surface.

I POINT

☐ If my cat skids or falls off a table, it leaves that table alone for several days. **I POINT**

☐ I frequently see my cat skid and fall off tables. But it always makes a second attempt. **2 POINTS**

☐ My cat skids if liquids are present, but it ultimately secures a foothold. **3 POINTS**

☐ My cat often climbs to a better vantage point before assessing the landing conditions. **4 POINTS**

☐ My cat is the Neil Armstrong of landers—undaunted by the state of any foreign surface. It never fails to secure a touchdown. **5 POINTS**

6

The Reflex

It's no coincidence that we refer to good physical reflexes as "catlike." "That goalie's like a cat," we say, and "Look at the catlike way I caught that mug as it tumbled from the cupboard!" But on the reflex scale, where does your cat rank?

Choose five different objects (varying in size, shape, color, and sound). Drop them, from differing heights, into the immediate vicinity of your cat—and be careful not to injure or annoy your pet in the process.

☐ It takes a while for my cat to be engaged by the falling object or objects. It is often a bit disinterested. **1 POINT**

☐ My cat follows the movement of the object with its eyes more regularly than moving its head or a limb toward it. **2 POINTS**

☐ My cat instinctively pounces at the object or bats it away with a forelimb. Home run. **3 POINTS**

☐ My cat says, "I concur—let's play," and then refuses to let me stop the reflex test until it is ready to stop. **4 POINTS**

☐ My cat instantly turns its attention to the falling object, but assesses the nature of the object before deciding whether or not to engage. **5 POINTS**

☐ In a split second, my cat finds a place from which to ambush the object. Its pupils enlarge, the claws emerge, and the item is "eliminated" before it touches the ground. **5 POINTS**

7

Herding the Humans

Once it has been introduced to a domestic environment, a cat gets to grips with the daily timetable of events very quickly—when you get up, have a shower, go to work, have your meals, and so on. It also figures out how its own feeding times are integrated into these daily routines.

MULTIPLE AWARD

Points are awarded for the ingenious ways in which your cat may attempt to either "accelerate" or "recalibrate" the timetable of the day, in order to bring forward the serving of cat food. You may include points for each of the tactics employed by your pet.

☐ THE DAILY MEWS: possibly the lowest form of human herding—your cat vocally moans (and moans) until you feed it. **1 POINT**

☐ STAND AND DELIVER: your cat stands in doorways, barring the entrance to "leisure areas" (such as the living room), forcing you to change tack and head for "cat-servicing" areas (such as the kitchen). **2 POINTS**

☐ HUMAN HURRIER: this slightly impatient tactic involves herding you in and out of rooms in order to fast-track the presentation of cat food. **3 POINTS**

☐ FACE-BATTING: your cat sits on your chest and bats your face with its paws until you pay attention to its immediate needs. **3 POINTS**

☐ THE AGENDA-BENDER: noticing that you've done some of the day's routines slightly out of order, your cat gets you back on track by herding you toward the kitchen, bathroom, or bedroom. **5 POINTS**

☐ THE CAT "IS" THE HAT: nothing alerts you to the presence of your cat—and its need to be fed—more than waking up to the warm, smothering sensation of an animal all over your head. **5 POINTS**

8

Cats and Trees: How Well Do They Mix?

To us, the backyard is a passive, sedate environment in which we can escape the rigors of the synthetic world with which we're obliged to interface. To a cat, the backdoor is a portal to a wilder dimension in which their dormant impulses can spring to life . . . or not.

Here's a yard-based challenge. When faced with a tree, does your cat do any of the following?

☐ NOT MY REMIT: your cat takes one look at the tree and dismisses it. **I POINT**

☐ BARKING UP THE WRONG ONE: your cat makes a valiant attempt to climb it, but ends up stranded, mid-trunk.
2 POINTS

☐ ABORT! ABORT!: your cat has scrambled its way into the lower branches, but its momentum is too great, which causes it to panic and abandon all progress. **3 POINTS**

☐ STEADY ASCENDER (AKA ASCEND AND BEFRIEND): noticing that another animal is already up in the tree, your cat embarks on a slow and steady climb. **4 POINTS**

☐ THE CROW'S NEST: your cat finds climbing trees a cinch and demonstrates this by sitting comfortably atop a high branch. **5 POINTS**

☐ THE CROW'S PEST: your cat climbs into trees with the express purpose of hassling birds or leaping down onto other unsuspecting victims. **5 POINTS**

Chapter Two

TERRITORIAL TESTS

Cats have three main goals in life: eat (as often as possible), reproduce (if necessary), and have a good time (as often as necessary). If they routinely wore clothes, they would shop around for T-shirts with slogans that say things like, "FEED ME," "DRAMA QUEEN," or "I'M A SEX KITTEN." And they would wear them with no hint of irony.

These central goals have made cats into highly territorial animals: they need to keep a tight rein on the geographical area in which they find their food and conduct their social interactions. Keeping cats as pets has introduced thousands of these beasts into the same urban, suburban, and rural environments, which means turf wars are constantly erupting.

This chapter will put you in the place of a Special Cat Squad agent, monitoring the local neighborhood for signs of conflict. And while you're at it, you can see how your own cat ranks in the local hierarchy—both inside your home and out there in the "OC," the badlands of Outdoor Catdom.

I

Wanderlust

This is an uncomfortable statistic for cat owners, but if your cat is sexually active (i.e., not neutered), it will roam around looking for action. In fact, unneutered males sometimes patrol territories that are up to ten times larger than those of sexually active females. If your cat has been "fixed" by the vet, to kick its sexual behavior to the curb, then the size of its territory will be dictated by the availability of food—and it will only get larger if the local nibbles become scarce.

How large is your cat's feeding territory?

☐ As long as there's food around, the cat rarely leaves the house. **1 POINT**

☐ The cat has to go out sometimes, because local cats come into our house and steal its food. **1 POINT**

☐ The cat eats in most days, but likes to eat out now and again. **2 POINTS**

☐ The cat eats at home and then goes next door for the second course. **3 POINTS**

☐ The cat's a continental scavenger, always eating al fresco. Only comes home to "top up" on food. **4 POINTS**

☐ Now and again, the cat will disappear for most of the day—and sometimes for several days. **4 POINTS**

☐ The cat is almost entirely independent of the home environment. **5 POINTS**

2

Strained Communication

Here's a stinking statistic: roughly one in ten domestic cats will urinate outside their litter box at some point in their lives, either to complain about some defect with the litter box or to make some other kind of statement. Cats can exist in groups (if they feel like it), but they can also choose to be totally independent and stake out their own territories, on either a permanent or "time-share" basis. This is why they leave their "pee" messages hither and thither. But what do they mean?

MULTIPLE AWARD

You can award points for any of the following statements routinely used by your cat.

TEST A: OUTSIDE THE HOME:

☐ CONSCIENTIOUS OBJECTOR: "There's a cat-on-cat conflict brewing around here, and I'm a bit nervous about it."
1 POINT

☐ GRAFFITI ARTIST: "I woz 'ere. Stayed for an hour. Got bored. Left." **2 POINTS**

☐ BACK IN FIVE: "I'm popping out briefly—leave a message and I'll get back to you ASAP." **3 POINTS**

☐ PLANNING PERMISSION: "I've applied to expand this bit of territory to improve my view of the park. Post your comments here." **3 POINTS**

☐ PROPERTY DEVELOPER: "This is my crib. If you use it, expect to be charged the appropriate rent—or evicted."
4 POINTS

TEST B: INSIDE THE HOME:

☐ A CRY FOR HELP: "I have emotional problems, and it's going to cost you a fortune in pet therapy to unock the deep well of my despair." **I POINT**

☐ THE VAGUE AVENGER: "You humans have annoyed me, but I'm not going to tell you why or how. Work it out."
2 POINTS

☐ PUT ME THROUGH TO THE MANAGER: "The state of this litter box is unacceptable. Please resolve and revert forthwith." **3 POINTS**

☐ IMMIGRATION ALERT: "You've introduced too many cats into the house. My territory is being compromised. You need to revise your immigration policy." **3 POINTS**

☐ I DIDN'T SEE THE MEMO: "You've made some structural and/or decorative changes in the house, and I did not approve them." **4 POINTS**

3

Turf Wars

The peaceful coexistence of the cats in your local neighborhood depends on the number of food outlets available. If there are lots of fast-food outlets serving each territory, with their garbage cans accessible—along with a generous scattering of insecure cat flaps among the local cat-loving population—then a state of harmony abounds. But if a snack shortage rears its ugly head, your cat may encounter insurgents and/or random pockets of resistance along the borders of its territory.

MULTIPLE AWARD

How does your cat deal with exterior territorial conflict? The behavior of your cat may depend on mitigating circumstances, so a set of options are included here for you to tick, as applicable.

☐ TOTAL ATOMIC REVERSAL: the cat shifts backward through the flap and into safety—very, very slowly, so as not to make a sound. **1 POINT**

☐ MILK MONITOR: the cat monitors the exterior environment until it's absolutely certain that no other cat is in the immediate vicinity. Then it makes an exit. **1 POINT**

☐ FLUPP–KER–CHUNNK–SKID–DUDH–DDDD–DDD: the cat scrams through the cat flap, terrified of a potential pursuit by its nemesis. **1 POINT**

☐ AIR RAID: tails are swishing, eyes are staring, and there's plenty of yowling in a standoff between your cat and another. Neither animal backs down until windows are opened to diffuse the tension. **3 POINTS**

☐ CAT BURGLAR/SNACK BURGLAR: your cat watches the next-door cat go out and then slinks into the neighboring cat flap. Post-invasion, it leaves a scent mark to say, "Thanks for the snack, Sucker." **4 POINTS**

☐ CONFIDENCE TRICKSTER/CONFIDENCE SNACKSTER: your cat chats up the next-door human, who has a microchip-operated cat flap for their cowardly pet. Your cat creeps in the door while their shields are down, sneaking off with some free food in a flash. All local cats now agree that your pet has the bragging rights. **6 POINTS**

4

Fight! Fight!! Fight!!!

Let's assume your cat is spoiling for a rumble in the urban (or suburban) jungle. Your cat is more than prepared to either defend its territory or penetrate the borders of another. What is his or her preferred style of claw-to-claw combat?*

---

*If your cat is a Conscientious Objector (see page 46), then all potential points are sadly forfeited.

MULTIPLE AWARD

☐ FACIAL THEATRICS: your cat hisses, spits, and bares its teeth—a good way of buying time while it decides whether to attack, defend, or flee. **2 POINTS**

☐ THE BOUFFANT BLUFF: your cat puffs up its tail and arches its back to make itself look huge, but ultimately backs away from any physical engagement. **2 POINTS**

☐ OPENING SHOT: your cat intimidates its opponent by slapping it with a paw (claws retracted) before the other cat has a chance to do the same. One-nil. **3 POINTS**

☐ CRAB CIRCLING: your cat engages its opponent in a lengthy face-off, involving some aggressive circling and side-to-side Flamenco stepping. **4 POINTS**

☐ FLIGHT CLUB: your cat often succeeds in forcing its opponent to exit the theater of conflict. **4 POINTS**

☐ CLUB SANDWICH: your cat often manages to get its opponent into a corner, so that its prey becomes the filling in a very unappetizing fur-knuckle sandwich. **5 POINTS**

5

Mastering the Cat Flap: aka Border Control

If the walls of your habitat are its political borders, than the cat flap at the back door is Border Control. Your cat is in a position to control the in–out flow of feline traffic—and there's nothing you can do about that, not without a referendum. A cat's jurisdiction over the immigration policy is known, in Europe, as *L'Art du Flappage*, and here are the ways in which your cat can score big points for your household—or not.

Your cat mainly uses a cat flap to:

☐ COME AND GO from the house at times that please the humans. **I POINT**

☐ ESCAPE from outdoor conflicts and incidences of domestic unrest (e.g., vacuuming). **I POINT**

☐ STARE at foreign cats from the safety of the kitchen. **2 POINTS**

☐ GROOM itself. The draft-excluding fringing of the flap's opening can be used to stimulate a fur coat or extract unwanted fluff. **3 POINTS**

☐ PUNCH other cats, by batting the flap outward (this earns a COMEDY GOLD bonus point). **5 POINTS**

☐ EXPRESS itself artistically. Mud and detritus can be smeared onto the window of the flap, in myriad creative ways, as the cat enters and exits. **5 POINTS**

☐ VISIT other homes for free meals, beds, toys, and EXTRA LOVE. **6 POINTS**

6

F.I.P.S. Feline Interior Patrol Systems

"It's the FBI—nobody move!"

Is your cat comfortable with human rules and regulations in the home? Or is your life increasingly wire-tapped and monitored by some kind of Feline Bureau of Investigation?

MULTIPLE AWARD

Watch out for the following modes of surveillance and reconnaissance.

☐ Your cat carries out a daily perimeter check of your home.
I POINT

☐ Your cat checks you over, thoroughly, each time you come in from work. This isn't affection—you are being inspected by Immigration Control. **2 POINTS**

☐ Your cat leaves objects strewn across the floor. As you nudge or move these items, your pet tracks your movements.
3 POINTS

☐ During periods of heightened security, your cat may implement a sequence of random dawn raids. You will be woken, abruptly, and intimately questioned. **4 POINTS**

☐ Your cat marks some rooms or objects with urine. This may mean it's locked in dispute with another animal or a member of the household that it's not happy with. It's possible you may have been "legally served with a writ."
5 POINTS

7

Soft Diplomacy: The Problem of the Uninvited Guest

As we've seen, the domestic cat can be a solitary and territorial animal. It is in its DNA. Its cousin, the Siberian tiger, claims about 190 square miles as its domain, and you wouldn't want to mess with it. Your cat may only want to claim the area from the washing machine to the front door as its primary lair—but still, don't go disrespecting that square footage. If visitors are scheduled, you need to be aware— using the scale overleaf—of how upsetting this may be for your pet.

When the doorbell rings, how does your cat usually respond?

☐ FLUPP–KER–CHUNNKK . . . (there goes the cat flap again). **1 POINT**

☐ A suitable (and normally fairly elevated) vantage point is found, from which the intruder can be glimpsed in absolute safety. **2 POINTS**

☐ 360-degree reconnaissance: the cat makes at least one full orbit of the guest or guests, maintaining a good distance. **3 POINTS**

☐ Familiarity breeds power—your cat goes straight in, spine luxuriantly arched, to reap some full-on stroking. **4 POINTS**

☐ Your cat leaps onto the visitor's shoulder (seemingly from nowhere) and uses its body as a "swab" for the extraction of a DNA sample. The sample is then taken away to the lab (situated just behind the washing machine) for analysis. **5 POINTS**

8

The Royal Order of the Clowder

You can refer to domestic cats collectively as a "clutter," a "glaring," or a "clowder." When they get together—either in the home or elsewhere—cats exhibit different levels of dominance, passivity, and submissiveness in relation to the other animals in the collective.*

---

* If you have several cats at home, you may need to observe each Test Subject one at a time, so that you can come up with the most accurate ratings for each member of the clowder.

With other cats present, how does your cat respond?

☐ INFERIORITY: at feeding times, the Test Subject is often interrupted by other cats attempting to eat from its bowl.
NIL POINTS

☐ INSECURITY: the Test Subject frequently seeks human contact or approval when other cats are around. **2 POINTS**

☐ INDEPENDENCE: if a room is occupied by other cats, the Test Subject often leaves to find its own space. **3 POINTS**

☐ INSOUCIANCE: if a younger or socially inferior cat attempts to mess with your cat, your pet is able to "pin" the other cat to the deck with one extension of a forelimb.
4 POINTS

☐ INCANDESCENCE: if the Test Subject is unhappy with the behavior of any other cat(s) in the group, it makes its feelings known through a short—but impactful—series of vocal protestations. **4 POINTS**

☐ IMPERIOUSNESS: when the Test Subject enters a room, other cats get up and move from the most comfortable rest areas, so your cat can "take the throne." **5 POINTS**

9

Seat of Power

Cats like to have the best of both worlds: they like to be free, but they also like to have territory and status in your home—two important things that you can provide, so long as you pay them "just enough" attention. Occasionally, a cat will remind you of your obligations to them by finding an item that is valuable to you and imposing themselves upon it. Their message is this: "No matter how important this thing is to you, right now, I will always be slightly more important."

MULTIPLE AWARD
Points are awarded for any of the following Acts of Appropriation.

☐ Sitting on the instructions for the flat-packed furniture you're sweating to put together. **2 POINTS**

☐ Sitting on the Allen wrench needed to construct the flat-packed furniture you're sweating to put together (see above). **2 POINTS**

☐ Sitting on an important job application (for longer, even, than you have). **3 POINTS**

☐ Sitting on the clothing that you'd laid out, ready to wear for the job interview (see above). **4 POINTS**

☐ Lying, spread-eagle, across the keyboard of an expensive laptop computer. **4 POINTS**

☐ Making a den inside the overnight bag brought over by a brand-new boyfriend or girlfriend. **5 POINTS**

10

Cat Colonialism

This test is an extension of Test Nine (see page 70), and you'll enjoy repeating it. Find a surface where you can mark out some kind of "temporary territory," (e.g., a circle made of rope or string, a chalked square on the floor of the garage, or a shape on the carpet made out of masking tape).

See how long it takes for your cat to sit in the middle of this fresh political boundary. Then, create more territories in different locations and repeat the experiment until you have a pretty good idea of your pet's response time.

☐ Zero engagement **NIL POINTS**

☐ 5 minutes **I POINT**

☐ I minute **2 POINTS**

☐ 30 seconds **3 POINTS**

☐ 10 seconds **4 POINTS**

☐ Less than 5 seconds **5 POINTS**

BONUS SECTION: While your cat is still engaged in this experiment, lay out several territories—in the same room or general location—and see which one your cat prefers. If it succeeds in choosing the largest territory, award your pet an extra point.

11

The Tao of Cats and Dogs

We've been conditioned over the years—through our exposure to cartoons such as Tom and Jerry, for example—that dogs and cats simply cannot coexist. Nevertheless, some households are progressive enough to have both hounds and felines on the premises, and they've survived intact. If you're one of these people who have both as pets . . . which beast rules the roost?

Here are some ways in which to observe the constantly evolving dynamic between your cat and its canine nemesis.

☐ CANIS MAJOR: there's a constellation of stars in the Southern Hemisphere known as Canis Major (the Greater Dog). It's written in the stars: your dog will always get the better of your cat. **NIL POINTS**

☐ NEVER THE TWAIN: your cat simply refuses to occupy a room if your dog is in it—or has been in it recently. **I POINT**

☐ DEMILITARIZED ZONES: your cat and dog have devised some kind of Unspoken Treaty, which stipulates that each one has total jurisdiction over certain areas of the house and/or yard. **2 POINTS**

☐ RESTRAINING ORDER: your cat uses snarls, hisses, and sharp teeth to keep your dog at a minimum distance of about 10 feet. **3 POINTS**

☐ AT EASE, SOLDIERS: your dog and cat worked out their differences long ago. They either coexist in sickening harmony, or just totally deny each other's existence. **4 POINTS**

☐ VELCRO LOCKDOWN: dogs often lunge toward cats—sometimes with violent intent, other times in a spirit of playfulness. Either way, your cat puts your dog in its place by gripping its hairy forelimbs with its own claws. Your dog struggles to retrieve its mitts. It has been roundly humiliated. **5 POINTS**

CHAPTER THREE

METEOROLOGY AND CAT COSMOLOGY

Cats generally keep their daily operations and interactions broad and flexible: they stay indoors when it suits them and take their business outside as and when appropriate. However, a lot of this feline flexibility depends on their ability to tolerate certain conditions that are—rather annoyingly—beyond their control, such as the weather, the rotation of the Earth, and the interaction of all physical matter in the universe.

One day, cats will have evolved to the point where they can influence these external conditions—but until then, they need to adapt to them. In this chapter, you can try and measure the extent to which your cat is aligned and "at one" with the greater universe beyond its own catdom.

Outdoor Precipitation

Ernest Hemingway once wrote a short story called "Cat in the Rain." The story observes a feline phenomenon: cats sometimes like to stay out in heavy rain, even though they do not necessarily enjoy getting wet. Hemingway's pithy, economical use of language neatly mirrors a cat's inherent efficiency—and its ability to stay out in all weather while simultaneously refusing to be affected by the atmospheric onslaught.

How does your cat respond as the rain starts to fall?

☐ HAIRY HOUDINI: vanishes to a warm, interior destination. End of story. **1 POINT**

☐ PAIN GAUGE: takes in the first few drops of rain, out of casual curiosity, but soon realizes its coat could turn into something very damp, matted, and cold. **2 POINTS**

☐ QUILTED JACKET: puffs out its insulating undercoat and heads to a more sheltered spot. **3 POINTS**

☐ WINDBREAKER: if the weather is blustery, the cat uses some kind of natural or artificial screen to avoid ruffled fur.
3 POINTS

☐ AMBIENT MOODS: finds shelter and tucks itself into an ultra-compact unit that no drip could possibly reach. The cat then calmly tunes into the "white noise" of the falling rain.
4 POINTS

☐ PRESCIENT PURR-MAKER: some time ago, the cat predicted it would rain and made all the necessary arrangements for a precipitation-free afternoon of nibbles and cocktails in the conservatory. **5 POINTS**

2

Indoor Precipitation

As responsible cat owners, we routinely protect our furry
critters from getting wet by offering them a warm, dry
domestic environment. That's all very nice, but in some cases
this does engender an aversion in your pet to all things moist.
You can find out just how wary your cat is by observing its
reaction to a showerhead or running faucet.

Which of the following best describes your cat's attitude to running water?

☐ RUNNING SCARED: bolts like lightning from any sign of liquid water. **NIL POINTS**

☐ PLUMBER'S MATE: will sit for hours watching a faucet, hoping to witness a trickle. **1 POINT**

☐ BED BATH: is quite happy to be patted down with a warm, damp cloth. **2 POINTS**

☐ SPLAT THE RAT: loves to try and bat the drips with a paw as they tumble out of the faucet. **3 POINTS**

☐ UNCOUTH CAT: the cat drinks from the faucet as often as it drinks from its bowl. **4 POINTS**

☐ WAR VETERAN: having fallen into water at least once, and survived to tell the tale, the cat is now comfortable with total immersion. **5 POINTS**

3

Crepuscular Critters

As humans, our field of vision extends to about 180 degrees, but, at an impressive 200 degrees, cats have a slightly broader view of the world. Also, their peripheral vision is superb: they are super-sensitive to animals or objects moving at the very limits of their visual range. Their eyes have many more "rod" cells, too, which means that their vision is much better than ours in lower levels of light.

MULTIPLE AWARD

All of this makes your cat a potentially active beast during the sinister, hunting hours of dawn, dusk, and darkness. Have you ever awoken to any of the following? Collect all the points that apply.

☐ A broken trinket (the result of clumsy nighttime hunter-gathering). **I POINT**

☐ A torn piece of fabric, clothing, or soft toy (which your cat has mistaken for a small living creature). **I POINT**

☐ A mysterious injury on your cat (the result of a mistimed lunge toward a small living creature). **I POINT**

☐ A dead mouse (or pieces thereof). **3 POINTS**

☐ More than one dead mouse, often witnessed as a "trail of gory carnage." **4 POINTS**

☐ A dead bird and/or an ornithological array of feathers lying in one place, but no cadaver. **5 POINTS**

4

Night School

Ah, the Darkness. It's a visiting friend that reaches out from the cosmos and paints a blank canvas of opportunity for every cat. Some cats embrace the night as a smorgasbord of exciting stuff to be devoured. Others are less thrilled by its unknowable othernesses. Where does your cat stand on this issue—on the rooftops or under the coffee table?

MULTIPLE AWARD

Which are your cat's favorite nighttime activities?
Make your observations and tick all the options
that apply.

☐ Sleeping (in addition to the daytime naps).
NIL POINTS

☐ Sex and/or socializing. **I POINT**

☐ Looking for a fight. **2 POINTS**

☐ Searching for scraps of food. **2 POINTS**

☐ Surveillance of the local neighborhood. **3 POINTS**

☐ Hunting for live prey to bring home as booty.
3 POINTS

5

Universal Enlightenment

Cats were revered in ancient Egypt. If anyone harmed a cat, they'd be in for a severe penalty. The Egyptians were also keen observers of the heavens—they believed in a sky goddess named Nut, whose body was said to be composed of stars. They also had a cat goddess, Bastet, the daughter of the sun god Ra.

So were the Egyptians on to something, do you think? Is there some kind of cosmic connection between your cat and the movement of the spheres? Does your cat know where the Higgs boson is?

MULTIPLE AWARD

☐ My cat never looks up at the sky. It is far too intimidated by the vast and unknowable extent of the Cosmos.

NIL POINTS

☐ My cat likes sitting out under a clear night sky, because it's a sure sign that it won't be raining any time soon.

I POINT

☐ My cat likes all things bright and spangly, including the moon and stars. **2 POINTS**

☐ My cat always pauses in front of the TV if it's showing a documentary about space. **3 POINTS**

☐ My cat seems to know exactly when the International Space Station will be passing overhead. **4 POINTS**

☐ My cat appears to administer an astronomy club for local felines. **5 POINTS**

☐ My cat does not need to look into the night sky. It already knows that the universe revolves around its own ego.

5 POINTS

Chapter Four

PSYCHOLOGICAL TESTS

Some cats are vocal and fairly direct in making their needs known—others less so. The meanings of their mewings are sometimes easy to comprehend (if they relate to food) and sometimes as cryptic as three-dimensional chess. Therefore, they also rely on other modes of behavior to give you a rough idea of their moods and motivations.

Is your cat an open book or a psychological Slinky that has become rather tangled? If it's the latter, the following tests and activities may help you demystify the four-footed enigma that trots around your home.

Feline Humility

Does your cat have a sense of humor? Cats appear to be kings and queens of slapstick, yet they frequently fail to comprehend their own comic genius.

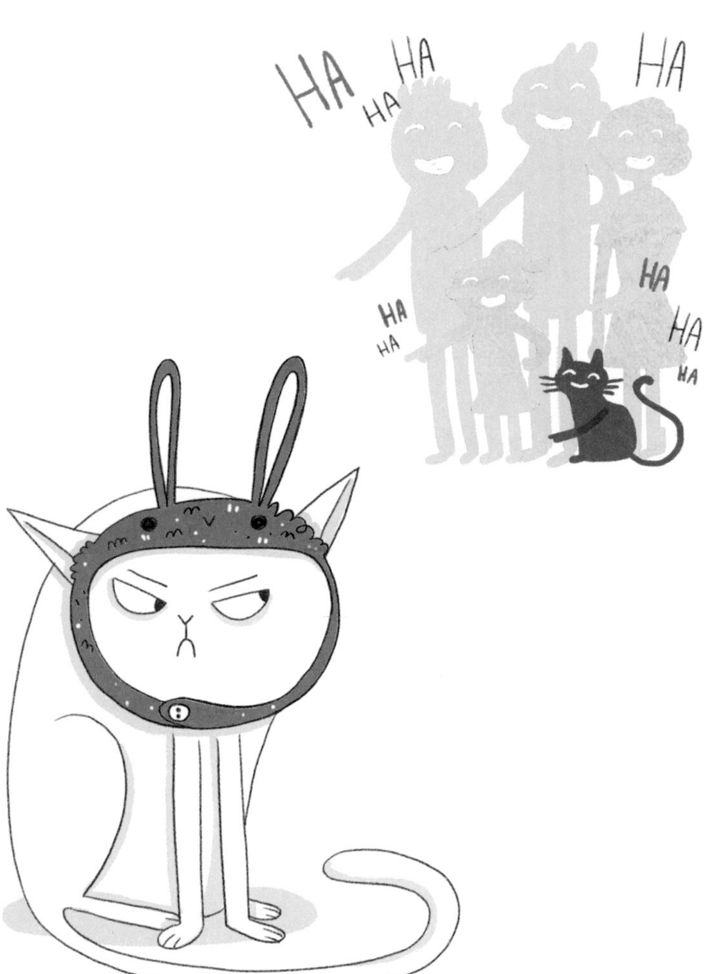
HA
HA
HA
HA
HA
HA
HA
HA
HA

Set up a harmless booby trap (e.g., arrange for soft items to fall as your cat opens a door, or make the kitchen floor a little bit slippery before it trots in for dinner). Then register your pet's default response to humiliation.

☐ My cat triggered the booby trap and immediately assumed it had unleashed ARMAGEDDON. I did not see the cat again for a few hours. **1 POINT**

☐ My cat made a sequence of vocal protestations after triggering the booby trap—possibly the cat equivalent of: "That wasn't funny. You're pathetic. Don't do that again."
2 POINTS

☐ My cat reacted to the booby trap, but then pretended that absolutely nothing had happened. **3 POINTS**

☐ My cat was initially startled, but saw the booby trap as a prelude to playtime. It shrugged off the humiliation in seconds. **4 POINTS**

☐ My cat glanced at the booby trap as it was triggered. Then it glanced at me, unleashed a withering look, and carried on with its day. **5 POINTS**

2

Fatal Attraction

Cats are often attracted to people who fundamentally do not like cats. What is this all about?

An ailurophobic (cat-fearing) friend of yours comes to visit. How does your cat respond to this person?

☐ My cat can see that my friend is not offering it eye contact. No eye contact = non-threatening, submissive behavior, so my cat feels comfortable when rubbing itself up against this new person. **3 POINTS**

☐ My cat perceives this person as the ultimate challenge, as it is not getting any attention from him or her. Therefore, my cat will not rest until it has achieved some kind of reaction, however violent that reaction might be. **4 POINTS**

☐ My cat has already succeeded in dominating the attention of everybody in the household, so whenever a new person arrives, that person must be assimilated into the feline hierarchy as quickly as possible. **5 POINTS**

3

TV Themes

All cats have sensitive hearing and fantastic eyesight. They see in both two and three dimensions and can distinguish between some colors. So there's no reason at all why they wouldn't enjoy Netflix. But what would be your cat's nightly viewing of choice?

MULTIPLE AWARD

When tested, does your cat pay particular attention to any of the following movie and TV categories*?

☐ Children's animation **1 POINT**

☐ Sitcom **1 POINT**

☐ TV news **2 POINTS**

☐ Political broadcast **3 POINTS**

☐ Historical documentary **4 POINTS**

☐ World cinema or film noir **5 POINTS**

---

*For the purpose of these tests, let us assume that your cat was able to stay focused on the TV screen for more than a minute at a time.

4

Treasure Hunt

Is your cat on your wavelength? Does it respond interactively to your behavior, or is it somewhat introspective—detached from you and focused, unilaterally, on its own internal streams of consciousness?

Scrunch up some shiny material or foil into balls of equal size. Hide them in places that your cat frequents around the house and yard. Does your cat ignore them or join the treasure hunt?

☐ My cat did not engage with a single bit of treasure. I had to retrieve them all after they'd started to gather dust.
NIL POINTS

☐ My cat noticed the hidden bits of treasure after a while, but wasn't really interested in them. **I POINT**

☐ My cat started to pull out or uncover the sparkly items, but soon got a little bored of the game. **2 POINTS**

☐ My cat discovered one or two shiny prizes, but abandoned the others because it was too busy batting the first ones around the room. **3 POINTS**

☐ My cat clearly got the idea and eventually discovered all of the sparkling bits of cat treasure. **4 POINTS**

☐ My cat discovered several of the foil balls, but steadfastly refused to uncover them all for fear of being labeled "a dog."
5 POINTS

5

Furry Dudes with
Low Moods

In all seriousness, a depressed cat is not a good thing. If your cat shows signs of having a low mood on a regular basis, you should take steps to try and identify the problem.*

---

* Please do take your cat for a checkup if it appears to be depressed. There could be an underlying medical problem. Also, your vet may be able to give you some tips for perking up your pet.

A NOTE ON SCORING

These scores work on an inverted scale: brief bouts of depression may show that your cat is sensitive, yet potentially able to recover its usual humor; low scores and point subtractions apply where there's evidence of a consistently low mood.

Is your cat . . .

☐ Neglecting its hygiene and self-grooming? **3 POINTS**

☐ Meowing and vocalizing more than usual? **3 POINTS**

☐ Making "protest sprays" across its litter box or in unusual places? **2 POINTS**

☐ Eating less or not eating at all some days? **2 POINTS**

☐ Hiding from you and avoiding interaction. **1 POINT**

☐ Becoming more aggressive, both physically and vocally?
SUBTRACT 1 POINT

6

Litter Box Semaphore

What's in your cat's litter box deposits? We're not talking about the chemical composition of your pet's feces and urine here. Nor are we talking about the state of its bank balance. We're talking about the psychological states that are communicated by the ways in which your cat adorns a plastic tray full of absorbent gravel.

MULTIPLE AWARD

Points are awarded for the successful communication of the following messages.

☐ I'M A LITTLE STRESSED: your cat has sprayed urine indiscriminately across the litter box or has left a stool or two just outside it. **1 POINT**

☐ THIS IS A DIRTY PROTEST: your cat makes a mess of its litter box because you've made a mess of its house.
2 POINTS

☐ I NEED AN EN SUITE, TOUT DE SUITE: if there are too many cats using the same litter box, your cat may stop using it until you provide something more private. **3 POINTS**

☐ CALL THE MAID: your cat refuses to use the litter box until you've rinsed it out and replaced all the litter granules.
4 POINTS

☐ I WOULD LIKE AN UPGRADE/RELOCATION: your cat may not be happy with the location of its litter box. It might start using it again if the tray has a superior vista, such as a sea view or a south-facing aspect. **5 POINTS**

7

The Slumber Challenge: Pushing the Boundaries of Deep Sleep

If your cat sleeps a lot, it may be a bit down in the dumps (see page 108), or it might just be a big fan of luxurious unconsciousness. In fact, if your cat is a champion sleeper, it may attract the attention of NASA—they're looking for people and animals that can cope with interstellar travel by spending most of the journey in a state of hypersleep. Maybe your cat should apply for the space program?

Points are awarded for the deepest hypersleepers, as follows.

My cat frequently sleeps for…

☐ 12 hours per day **2 POINTS**

☐ 12–14 hours per day **3 POINTS**

☐ 14–16 hours per day **5 POINTS**

☐ 16–18 hours per day **2 POINTS**

☐ 18–20 hours per day (i.e., whenever it's not eating)*
1 POINT

---

* Although this is an impressive bit of slumber, excessive sleep could also be an indicator that all is not well with your pet. So if this kind of sleep seems uncharacteristic, please refer the animal to an expert.

Chapter Five

SUPERNATURAL TESTS

Cats exert an enigmatic, strange, and preternatural hold over us humans. Is this a true phenomenon or just something that we've created in our minds?

Ever since we first domesticated them, we have associated cats with things that are otherworldly . . . the ancient Egyptians elevated them to a godlike status and protected them under the laws of their civilization. But then came the wicked backlash. Things very much turned against the growing feline population in the middle ages, when people began to associate cats with paganism, devil worship, and witchcraft. In some parts, domestic cats were feared as the bringers of bad fortune and driven out of people's homes in troubled times.

As a hangover of this, we still see cats in a somewhat sinister or supernatural light. But perhaps this is what we truly want to believe. It is, after all, quite a wonderful notion: the idea that cats can provide us with a psychic link to another world—the realm of the paranormal.

Old Wives' Tails [sic]

The world is awash with cat-related superstitions. How many of the following old wives' tales does your cat confirm through its behavior?

MULTIPLE AWARD

Points can be collected for each scenario you have observed.

☐ BLACK HUMOR: I have a black cat. It deliberately plays on people's superstitions by crossing their path and taunting them until they have to chase it away. **2 POINTS**

☐ CAT–CHOO, WA–HOO!: whenever I overhear my cat sneezing, I seem to have a day full of lucky occurrences. **2 POINTS**

☐ KAT KARMA: if ever I mistreat my cat, several days of bad luck follow. **2 POINTS**

☐ WET WEATHER REPORT: it often rains just after my cat has washed behind its ears. **2 POINTS**

☐ BETRAYAL BULLETIN: whenever I dream about my cat, I know that treachery is afoot. **3 POINTS**

2

Pets and the Paranormal

Let's cut straight to the chase: can your cat see dead people?

MULTIPLE AWARD

☐ We had another cat, which died. Our new cat seems to spend a lot of time staring at and circling the places where our old cat used to sit and sleep. **2 POINTS**

☐ My cat behaves very differently on consecrated ground. **3 POINTS**

☐ My cat sometimes stares at a single spot in the room or on the ceiling and starts spitting and hissing. Then, after a while, it suddenly reverts to its normal behavior. **4 POINTS**

☐ My cat appears to sense things before they happen—for example, it'll move or leave the room just before someone knocks over a hot beverage. **4 POINTS**

☐ My cat often stares at an area of the house—such as the stairs—and appears to follow the movement of an unseen being moving back and forth, up and down. **5 POINTS**

3

Stare-ology

Just how psychically powerful are your cat's stares?

MULTIPLE AWARD

Points can be awarded for each occular occurence observed.

☐ In a staring contest between two cats, my cat is usually the one to walk away. **NIL POINTS**

☐ By staring at them, my cat can make my other pets leave the room. **2 POINTS**

☐ If I'm eating, and my cat stares at me, I lose my appetite immediately. **2 POINTS**

☐ My cat is rarely the loser in a cat-to-cat stare-off.
3 POINTS

☐ A friend once felt so intimidated by my cat's stares that he/she had to leave the house. **4 POINTS**

☐ My cat can wake me from a deep sleep, just by staring at me. **5 POINTS**

☐ My cat can stare at objects and make them levitate.
100 POINTS

4

Year of the Cat

Does your cat live up to and/or exploit the typical characteristics of its star sign?

Pisces

Leo

Taurus

Maximum points are awarded for a positive match in each case.

☐ ARIES (March 21–April 20): a temperamental cat that often uses a certain amount of Feline Force to get its own way. **5 POINTS**

☐ TAURUS (April 21–May 21): this cat is relatively unflappable, but dislikes change. **5 POINTS**

☐ GEMINI (May 22–June 21): a playful, fickle, interminably youthful feline. **5 POINTS**

☐ CANCER (June 22–July 23): shy, evasive, enigmatic, and emotionally complex. **5 POINTS**

☐ LEO (July 24–August 23): an overly pampered and pretentious egomaniac. **5 POINTS**

☐ VIRGO (August 24–September 23): a fastidious and self-preening pet, but ultimately a very satisfying member of the household. **5 POINTS**

☐ LIBRA (September 24–October 23): vain and slightly insecure, this cat demands a lot of attention and affection.

5 POINTS

☐ SCORPIO (October 24–November 22): a mean-spirited, powerful, vengeful beast! **5 POINTS**

☐ SAGITTARIUS (November 23–December 22): a dreamy enigma—appearing and disappearing on a whim.

5 POINTS

☐ CAPRICORN (December 23–January 20): serious, shy, selfish, determined—and always right. **5 POINTS**

☐ AQUARIUS (January 21–February 19): the melancholy poet of all cats—constantly bored or evasive, seeking change and cultural stimulation. **5 POINTS**

☐ PISCES (February 20–March 20): a complex, shape-shifting, inconsistent, and ultimately unknowable animal.

5 POINTS

The Scores

PHYSICAL TESTS: ANALYSIS
Lower range: 9–37
Your cat is not a physically imposing creature. It is happy to sit back and let you set the agenda. Watch out for signs of continued disinterest and withdrawal—you may have a depressed animal on your hands.

Median range: 38–67
This cat likes to get involved. It has a healthy attitude to fun. It has clearly engaged with the tests and scores consistently well in them, as long as it's in the mood.

Genius range: 68 and above
Okay, careful now: this animal is straight off the set of James Bond, where it has been cast as the greatest nemesis 007 has ever faced. This is one physically self-assured and confident cat. Brace yourself for the day when it demands to have its own Winnebago somewhere on your property.

How your cat could improve
The more you engage with your cat on a physical level, the more you will come to know its levels of confidence and contentment in this arena. Every cat is different: some are content to sit aside from the rough-and-tumble of life, while others become more open and physically interactive over time. By repeating these tests every once in a while, you can find out if your cat is in the latter category.

TERRITORIAL TESTS: ANALYSIS
Lower range: 11–67
Essentially a house cat, this animal feels more relaxed and confident indoors than it does outdoors.

Median range: 68–119
Your cat is well known in the local area, but it doesn't push its luck. It's winning the battle for hearts and minds both at home and abroad and is always ready to negotiate when it comes to a territorial dispute.

Genius range: 120 and above
This cat is constantly pushing boundaries and expanding its sphere of influence. Unbeknownst to you, it may already have invaded and conquered several neighboring properties, displacing countless house cats in the process. Look out for feline refugees.

How your cat could improve
If your cat is in the Median or Genius range, you may find it will continue to experiment with ways of asserting itself. This may result in an accumulation of territorial gains—and hence a greater points score—as time goes on. But if your cat is more content with its boundaries as they are, the scores should remain fairly consistent.

METEOROLOGY AND COSMOLOGY TESTS: ANALYSIS
Lower range: 4–25
Your cat clings to the comforts offered by domesticity. It has turned its back on the unknowable wilds of outdoor living.

Median range: 26–47
This cat enjoys the thrill of the outdoors and also perceives its indoor world as something to be tamed and mastered.

Genius range: 48 and above
The spirits of its feline ancestors run through this cat. It is in touch with its wilder elements and looks upon the world with a philosophical eye. You could learn a great deal from this animal.

How your cat could improve
Your cat was born a certain way, and you've (hopefully) grown to love its personality. You can't really train a cat to be more aware of its broader environment if—deep down—it is content with the limits of its universe. So you'll probably find little change in the results of repeated assessments. But who knows? Introducing your cat to new things is always interesting.

PSYCHOLOGICAL TESTS: ANALYSIS
Lower range: 9–27
You need to keep an eye on this one. Its withdrawn, secretive behavior might just be an aspect of its personality—or it could be the sign of some underlying problem or depression.

Median range: 28–42
You have no cause for concern here. This is a well-balanced animal that's reasonably content in its own furry skin. It knows how to be happy, and it'll let you know when it's "not amused."

Genius range: 43 and above
This cat is self-assured to the point of frustration. There are times when it doesn't really see the point of humans (except as contributors to the food supply), and this may be upsetting for its so-called "owners."

How your cat could improve
As with Chapter Three, there's probably not a lot you can do about your cat's innate personality—but there may be some aspects of its overall psychology that you can address. If you have a cat from a rescue home or a previous owner, there may be some underlying issues (from the animal's early years) that have affected its confidence. By spending more time with the animal and exposing it, gradually, to some of the things it seems to be uncomfortable with (such as people or other pets), you might find that its psychological scores will improve over time.

SUPERNATURAL TESTS: ANALYSIS
Lower range: 4–14
Whatever's out there in the spirit world, your cat is either ignoring or blissfully unaware of it.

Median range: 15–49
Your cat is obviously quite sensitive to certain phenomena and can use its own psychological strengths to its advantage. The balance is right: the animal's extra-sensory and/or paranormal awareness is reassuring, rather than terrifying.

Genius range: 50 and above

Your cat is part of something bigger and more profound than you could possibly imagine. It could even be the gatekeeper to another dimension. Keep watching.

How your cat could improve

There's no changing the results of this one. The behavior will be deep-rooted and fixed by now. Check the Yellow Pages for a reasonably priced exorcist and just hang on to your sanity as best as you can

OVERALL ANALYSIS

Lower range: 35–174

If clingy cats are your thing, then don't worry if your pet falls into this category. Some cats are more dependent on their owners than others and like to be indoors a lot more, and this is merely part of the feline world's rich demographic. You'll only have cause for concern if your cat consistently shows signs of aggression, distress, or social withdrawal. All joking aside, you should seek an expert's opinion on these types of behaviors.

Median range: 175–328

Cats that score in this range are (generally speaking) the kind of animals that are a joy to live with. They are comfortable around humans in the home and see you as a central cog in the complex machinations of their universe. But they will follow their natural instincts and wander astray from time to time. It's healthy for a cat to have broad horizons and be curious about the world outside, so this shouldn't worry you.

Genius range: 329 and above

This is a sophisticated, independent, and well-adapted beast that has found ways of pleasing itself in pretty much every environment it finds itself in. It's not necessarily the best kind of cat to own, but nevertheless this animal deserves your respect and admiration. Enjoy this superior specimen while you can—because as soon as it grows that opposable thumb it has always wanted, this cat will no longer need you.

ACKNOWLEDGMENTS

I am sincerely grateful to my great friend and eminent cat-sultant, Carron Brown, for suggesting several of the tests in this book, and for making sure that my observations of cat behavior are reasonably accurate. I have tried to make this book as fun as possible, while (hopefully) being a useful tool for getting to know your animal a lot better, and Carron has been a great help. I also need to acknowledge my former landlady, Lisa Thomas, for giving me all the experience of cats I'll ever need. Thanks go to the Brown family (Lola Mae, George Murray, and Shannon) for pet-bunk inspiration. My thanks, also, to Caitlin Doyle for her continued efforts to bring domestic animals to the forefront of nonfiction publishing. Caitlin, these animals salute you with furry forelimbs of fun. Keep up the good work.

The General Certificate of Feline Excellence

This certifies that

_____

has participated in a series of tests designed to measure his/her

aptitude in respect of the following categories:

Physical prowess:	☐	☐
Territorial command:	☐	☐
Cosmological mind-set:	☐	☐
Psychological strength:	☐	☐
Supernatural sensitivity:	☐	☐

TOTAL GRADE ☐ ☐

EXAMINER'S SIGNATURE _____

DATE _____